10-minute
Reading
and
Writing

but and or until

Capital letters

1 Underline the nouns that need capital letters.

pirate   water

africa   james

2 Circle the letters that should be capital letters in these sentences.

a parrot ruffled her feathers.

the chest was full of gold coins.

where is sam?

3 Answer the questions below using full sentences. Check your capital letters.

What is your name?

_____

What country do you live in?

_____

4 Circle the letters that should be capital letters in the story.

the pirate ship set sail across the ocean. captain jones was very excited. they were off to find buried treasure!

Punctuation

1 Complete each sentence with a period.

A period is used at the end of a sentence that isn't a question.

The cauldron bubbled_

The wizard cast a spell_

The wand sparkled with magic_

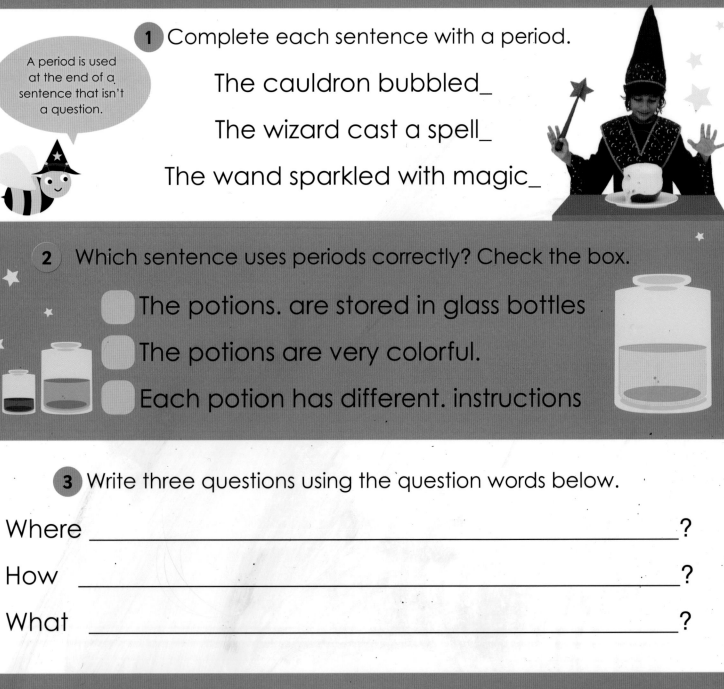

2 Which sentence uses periods correctly? Check the box.

☐ The potions. are stored in glass bottles

☐ The potions are very colorful.

☐ Each potion has different. instructions

3 Write three questions using the question words below.

Where _____?

How _____?

What _____?

4 Choose the correct punctuation to go at the end of each sentence.

·   ·   ?

This is a magic frog ___

Its name is Freddie ___

What sound does a frog make ___

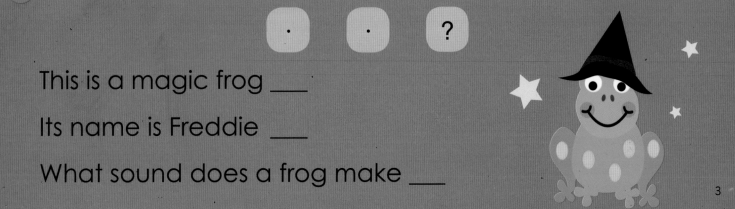

Adjectives

An adjective is a word that describes a noun.

1 Think of an adjective to describe each picture.

puppy   sun   flower   ring

Soft _____   _____   _____   _____

2 Choose one adjective to complete each sentence.

new   loud   hot

That puppy's bark is _____ .

It was _____ at the park today.

I bought my dog three _____ toys.

3 Can you put this sentence in order?

little at barked The me puppy .

_____

4 Underline the adjectives.

The puppy ran through the long grass, her soft

ears flapping across her brown eyes. She dashed

behind a little green bush and barked.

Nouns

A noun is a person, place, or object.

1 Circle the other two words that are nouns.

pretty (lollipop) tasty   coin   bag

2 Complete these sentences with your own nouns.

I put on my _____ and walked to the store.

Inside were all my favorite treats. There were

_____ and _____ .

3 Look around you. Write down six nouns that you can see.

_____   _____

_____   _____

_____   _____

4 Underline the two words that should have capital letters because they are names.

texas town emma

candy wrapper

Sight words

1 Circle the words that are spelled correctly to describe what the robots are doing.

push

poosh

poul

pull

2 Choose the right words to complete the conversation.

said   I   today   school   Where

"Hello!" _____ Robot Rosa.

"_____ are you going _____?" said Bolt.

"_____ am going to _____," said Robot Rosa.

3 Find and circle the sight words in the sentences below. Count how many times you spot each one, and then write the number in the correct box.

The park is full of happy robots. Some of the robots are jumping and some of the robots are skipping.

the ◯ is ◯ full ◯ some ◯ are ◯

Missing words

1 Choose the correct word to complete each sentence.

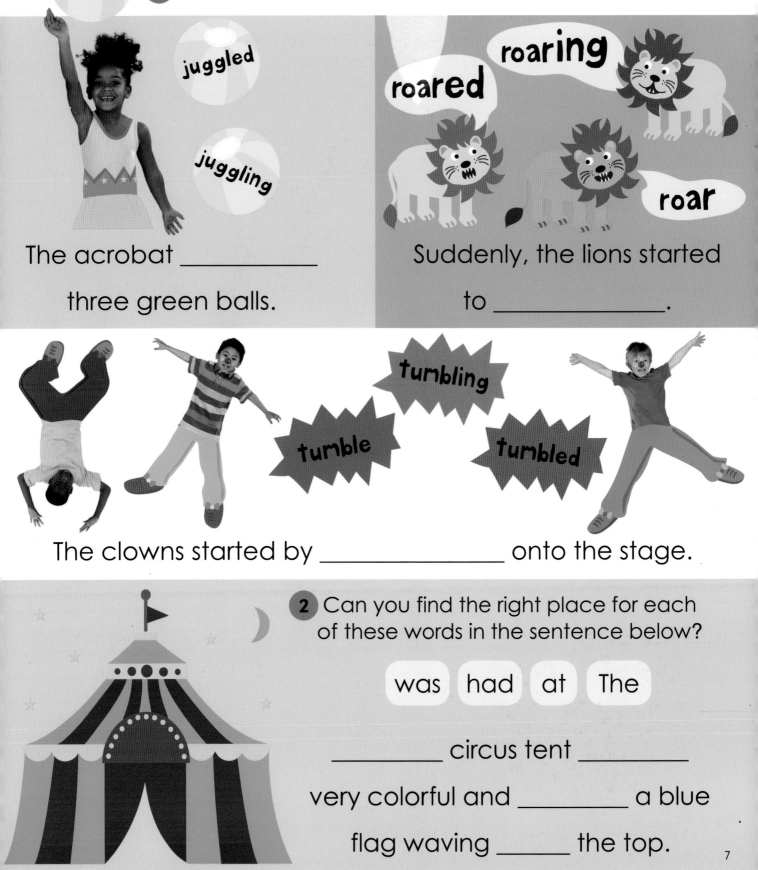

juggled

juggling

roaring

roared

roar

The acrobat _____ three green balls.

Suddenly, the lions started to _____.

tumbling

tumble

tumbled

The clowns started by _____ onto the stage.

2 Can you find the right place for each of these words in the sentence below?

was   had   at   The

_____ circus tent _____

very colorful and _____ a blue

flag waving _____ the top.

Comprehension

Read the cake recipe, and then answer the questions below.

Cake Recipe

4 eggs   1 cup butter

2 cups flour 2 cups sugar

1. Beat the eggs in a glass bowl.
2. Add the flour, sugar, and butter, and mix together.
3. Pour the mixture into a cake pan.
4. Bake in the oven for thirty minutes at 350°F.
5. Once out of the oven, let the cake cool for ten minutes.
6. Decorate the cake.

1 What sort of bowl do you need?

metal   wooden   glass

2 Using numbers, not words, how long does it take to . . .

Bake the cake? _____ minutes

Cool the cake? _____ minutes

3 Circle the ingredients that are in the recipe.

flour   chocolate

eggs   butter

sponge   sugar

4 Put the instructions in the correct order by writing 1, 2, or 3 in each box.

 Decorate the cake.

Beat the eggs.

Pour into a pan.

Adjectives

1 What is an adjective? Underline the correct answer.

an action word   the name of a place   a describing word

2 Check the best adjective to describe each noun.

	fast	hot	blue
rocket	○	○	○
planet	○	○	○
sun	○	○	○

3 Read these adjectives, and then add them into the story below.

green   strange   old   tall   gloomy   crumbling

The _____ planet was home

to _____ creatures. They lived in

an _____ castle. The _____

towers rose high above its _____ walls.

A path led up to the _____ gate.

Can you swap the adjectives? Wipe away
your first answers and give it a try!

Story sentences

1 Draw lines to make three complete sentences.

The cat drank water because   it was fun.

The kitten played because   he was soft.

I stroked the cat because   she was thirsty.

2 Use these words to complete the two sentences below.

| tiny | basket | jumped | branch |

The cat _____ onto the _____ .

Curled up in the _____ was a _____ kitten.

3 Write out each sentence again so that it makes sense.

The   licked   hand   my   cat   .

_____

explored   kitten   A   garden   the   .

_____

4 Put this story in order by writing 1, 2, 3, or 4 in each box.

◯   No longer hungry, she went back to sleep.

◯   She stretched and went to find her breakfast.

◯   The kitten woke up in her basket.

◯   The kitten found her bowl and ate everything!

Phonics

1 Complete the crossword using the picture clues.

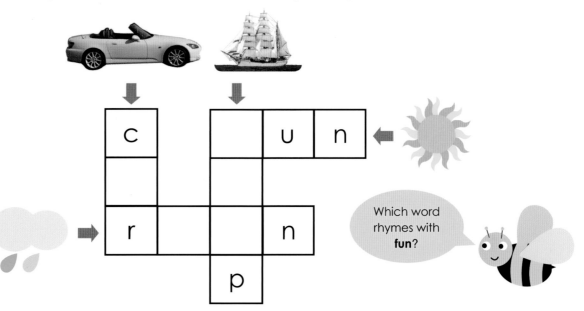

Which word rhymes with **fun**?

2 Circle the three words that can be changed into new words by adding a final **e**. Say the new words out loud.

plan   truck   car   train   kit

3 Pick the correct sounds for each word and write it out.

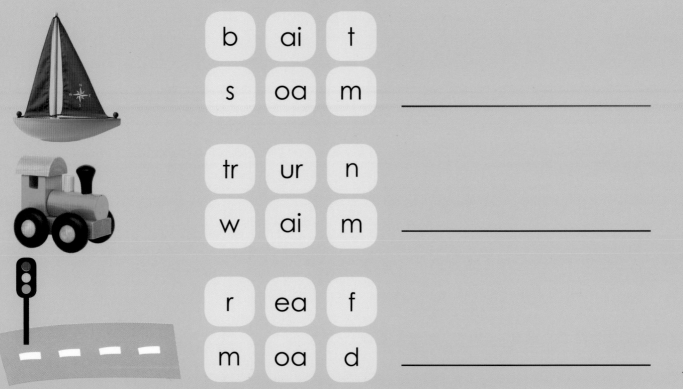

b ai t
s oa m   _____

tr ur n
w ai m   _____

r ea f
m oa d   _____

Conjunctions

1 Choose the correct word from below to complete the sentence in each car.

but   because   and   but   and

A conjunction is a word that links two parts of a sentence together.

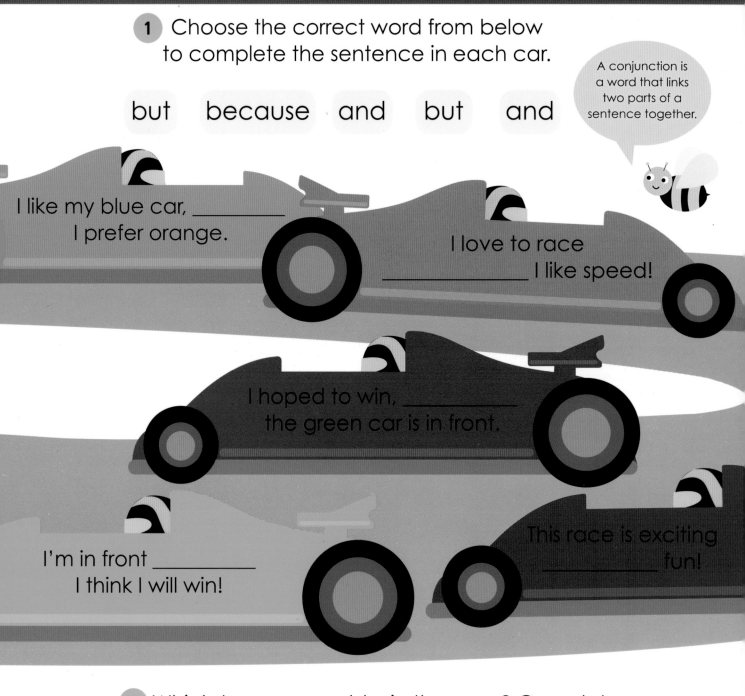

I like my blue car, _____ I prefer orange.

I love to race _____ I like speed!

I hoped to win, _____ the green car is in front.

I'm in front _____ I think I will win!

This race is exciting _____ fun!

2 Which two cars could win the race? Complete the sentence with the colors and the reason.

I think the winner could be _____ or

_____ because _____

_____ .

Comprehension

Bear was having a very busy day in the playroom. He had cleaned up the wooden blocks and was dusting the bookshelf when, suddenly, he remembered it was Giraffe's birthday.

Bear gathered all the toys together and asked, "What shall we do to surprise Giraffe?"

Dinosaur suggested they bake a chocolate cake.

"Giraffes don't like cake!" cried Daisy Doll. The toy soldiers agreed.

"Why don't we throw her a party?" suggested Delilah Doll. All the toys thought this was a great idea and went to work.

1 Read the story and answer the following questions.

What is the setting of the story? _____

Who remembered Giraffe's birthday? _____

2 Which characters think giraffes don't like cake? Circle the correct answers.

Delilah Doll   Bear   the toy soldiers   Daisy Doll

3 Put the story in order by writing 1, 2, 3, or 4 in each box.

Bear cleans up the blocks.

Delilah suggests a party.

Dinosaur suggests baking a cake.

Bear remembers Giraffe's birthday.

Phonics

1 Use the sounds below to make three words.

ch   o   i   sh   p   n

_____

_____

_____

2 Use **th** and **ch** to complete this question.

Do you ___ink the moon is made of ___eese?

3 Use **sh**, **wh**, **th**, and **ch** to complete the words in these sentences.

___e mouse was ___ased by a cat ___at wanted to cat___ him. He jumped into a ___oe, ___ich hid him from ___e cat.

4 In some words, **er**, **ir**, **or**, or **ur** can make the same sound. Find the five words with this sound in the word search.

Read each word out loud to hear the **er** sound.

l	a	d	d	e	r	t	s
e	v	b	c	i	s	o	b
n	p	i	h	y	n	g	i
w	e	c	u	f	l	m	r
h	w	o	r	d	e	t	d
k	g	e	t	o	x	f	o
n	i	s	h	i	r	t	l

ladder

bird

hurt

word

shirt

14

Comprehension

Read the text and answer the questions below.

The audience sat down for the third act of the play. The red velvet curtains opened to reveal a ballroom where people in fine clothes were dancing. Cinderella looked beautiful in her blue ball gown. Her silver tiara sparkled under the light of the chandelier hanging from the ceiling.

Suddenly, the giant clock on the wall struck midnight. Cinderella gasped in horror and ran off the stage. Prince Charming hurried after her, his gold cloak flapping over his shoulders. Cinderella had left her slipper behind!

The curtains closed as the audience cheered loudly.

1 What does this piece of writing describe? Check the answer:

- ⊗ A play about Cinderella
- ◯ A poem about Cinderella
- ◯ A letter to Cinderella

2 What did Cinderella leave onstage? Check the answer.

- ◯ Her cape
- ◯ Her slipper
- ◯ Her hat

3 Who cheered loudly?

_____

4 What is the setting of the play?

_____

Sight words

1 Circle the word that is spelled correctly in each pair.

freind   friend

houss   house

where   wher

theer   there

Sight words are hard to sound out, so you have to remember the spellings!

2 Can you unscramble these words?
The first letter has been done for you.

I swa   w_____ eating my lunch.

I elvo   l_____ food!

We always sit ehre   h_____ at dinnertime.

3 Count how many times you spot each word below in these sentences, and then write the number in the correct box.

My favorite food is pizza. What is your favorite food?

My friend likes bell peppers on her pizza, but she has a

brother who only likes ham on his pizza. I like to share my

food. Do you like to share your food with your friend?

your   ⬭   his   ⬭   my   ⬭

she   ⬭   you   ⬭   I   ⬭

16

Phonics

1 Complete the crossword using the picture clues.

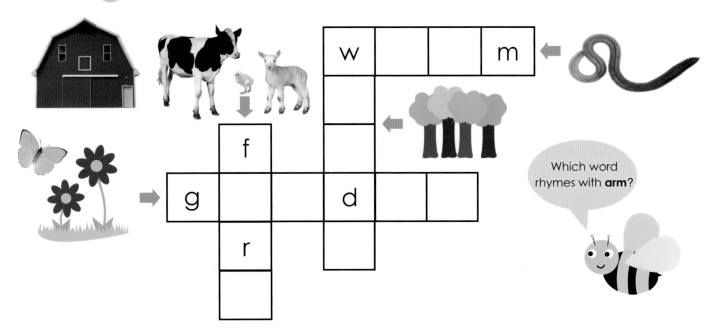

2 Which two words from the crossword have the **ar** sound?

_____   _____

3 Pick the correct sounds for each word and write it out.

Comprehension

Read the paragraph, and then answer the questions below.

Owls live alone and hunt at night. They have large eyes, which are much better than ours at seeing in the dark. Owls have sharp talons, strong beaks, and lightweight feathers. Their feathers help them move silently in the air when they fly so that their prey won't hear them coming. Some common owl species are barn owl, snowy owl, and spotted owl.

wings →

eyes

beak

talons →

1. What is the main topic of this text?

2. When do owls hunt?

3. Are owls' talons sharp or smooth?

4. Why do owls fly silently?

_____

_____

_____

_____

5. Which is the correct list of common owl species?

○ black, ginger, and tabby

○ barn, snowy, and spotted

○ clown, gold, and star

Conjunctions

1 Circle the trains with conjunctions on them.

but   and   or   now

2 Write in the correct word to complete each sentence.

or   until   and

The train would not move _____ the whistle was blown.

Would you like to travel north _____ south today?

The train was blue _____ had a number on the side.

3 Cross out the conjunction that is wrong in each sentence.

The clock chimed and   if we climbed aboard the train.

The train driver smiled because   or she was happy.

I had to rush until   so I would not miss my train.

Prefixes and suffixes

1 Add the suffix **ing** to each word to show what each turtle is doing.

These are all action words.

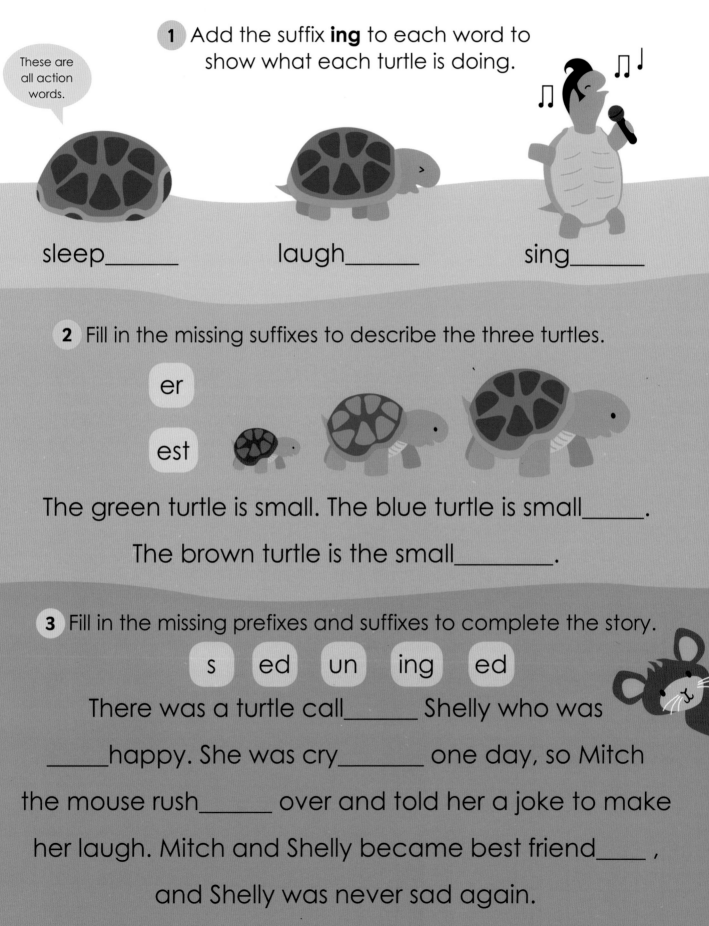

sleep_____   laugh_____   sing_____

2 Fill in the missing suffixes to describe the three turtles.

er

est

The green turtle is small. The blue turtle is small_____.

The brown turtle is the small_____.

3 Fill in the missing prefixes and suffixes to complete the story.

s   ed   un   ing   ed

There was a turtle call_____ Shelly who was

_____happy. She was cry_____ one day, so Mitch

the mouse rush_____ over and told her a joke to make

her laugh. Mitch and Shelly became best friend____ ,

and Shelly was never sad again.

Answers

There are word games and flash cards at the back of the book.

Page 2 – Capital letters
1. Africa   James
2. Ⓐ parrot ruffled her feathers.
   Ⓣhe chest was full of gold coins.
   Ⓦhere is Ⓢam?
4. Ⓣhe pirate ship set sail across the ocean. Ⓒaptain Ⓙones was very excited. Ⓣhey were off to find buried treasure!

Page 3 – Punctuation
1. The cauldron bubbled.
   The wizard cast a spell.
   The wand sparkled with magic.
2. The potions are very colorful.
4. This is a magic frog ⊙
   Its name is Freddie ⊙
   What sound does a frog make ⊘

Page 4 – Adjectives
1. *Examples*:
   bright sun   **pretty** flower   **sparkly** ring
2. That puppy's bark is **loud**.
   It was **hot** at the park today.
   I bought my dog three **new** toys.
3. The little puppy barked at me.
4. *Adjectives*: long   soft   brown   little   green

Page 5 – Nouns
1. coin   bag
4. *These words need capital letters*: Texas, Emma

Page 6 – Sight words
1. push   pull
2. "Hello!" **said** Robot Rosa.
   "**Where** are you going **today**?" said Bolt.
   "I am going to **school**," said Robot Rosa.

3. the ③ is ① full ① some ② are ②

Page 7 – Missing words
1. juggled   roar   tumbling
2. **The** circus tent **was** very colorful and **had** a blue flag waving **at** the top.

Page 8 – Comprehension
1. glass
2. Bake the cake: **thirty** minutes.
   Cool the cake: **ten** minutes.
3. flour   eggs   butter   sugar
4.   1 Beat the eggs.
     2 Pour into a pan.
     3 Decorate the cake.

Page 9 – Adjectives
1. Adjective: a describing word
2. rocket: *fast*   planet: *blue*   sun: *hot*

Page 10 – Story sentences
1. The cat drank water because she was thirsty.
   The kitten played because it was fun.
   I stroked the cat because he was soft.
2. The cat **jumped** onto the **branch**.
   Curled up in the **basket** was a **tiny** kitten.
3. The cat licked my hand.
   A kitten explored the garden.
4. 1 The kitten woke up in her basket.
   2 She stretched and went to find her breakfast.
   3 The kitten found her bowl and ate everything!
   4 No longer hungry, she went back to sleep.

Page 11 – Phonics
1.

c		s	u	n
a		h		
r	a	i	n	
		p		

2. plane   care   kite
3. boat   train   road

Page 12 – Conjunctions

1. *blue car*: but *orange car*: because
   red car: but *purple car*: and
   green car: and
2. *Example*: I think the winner could be green
   or red because they are nearest to the
   finish flag.

Page 13 – Comprehension

1. the playroom Bear
2. Daisy Doll and the toy soldiers
3. 1 Bear cleans up the blocks.
   2 Bear remembers Giraffe's birthday.
   3 Dinosaur suggests baking a cake.
   4 Delilah suggests a party.

Page 14 – Phonics

1. *Possible words*:
   chip chop chin ship shop
   shin nip pin
2. Do you **th**ink the moon is made of **ch**eese?
3. The mouse was chased by a cat that
   wanted to catch him. He jumped into a
   shoe, which hid him from the cat.

4.

l	a	d	d	e	r	t	s
e	v	b	c	i	s	o	b
n	p	i	h	y	n	g	i
w	e	c	u	f	l	m	r
h	w	o	r	d	e	t	d
k	g	e	t	o	x	f	o
n	i	s	h	i	r	t	l

Page 15 – Comprehension

1. A play about Cinderella
2. Her slipper
3. The audience
4. A ballroom

Page 16 – Sight words

1. friend   house
   where   there
2. I **was** eating my lunch.
   I **love** food!
   We always sit **here** at dinnertime.
3. your 3 his 1 my 3 she 1 you 1 I 1

Page 17 – Phonics

1.

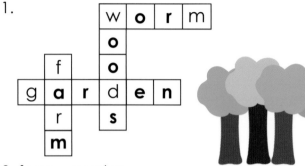

		w	o	r	m
		o			
	f	o			
g	a	r	d	e	n
	r	s			
	m				

2. f**ar**m   g**ar**den
3. snail   farmer   leaf

Page 18 – Comprehension

1. owls
2. at night
3. sharp
4. Owls fly silently so that their
   prey won't hear them coming.
5. barn, snowy, and spotted

Page 19 – Conjunctions

1. but   and   or
2. The train would not move **until**
   the whistle was blown. Would you like to
   travel north **or** south today? The train was
   blue **and** had a number on the side.
3. The clock chimed **and** we climbed
   aboard the train. The train driver smiled
   because she was happy. I had to rush **so**
   I would not miss my train.

Page 20 – Prefixes and suffixes

1. sleep**ing**   laugh**ing**   sing**ing**
2. The green turtle is small. The blue turtle is
   small**er**. The brown turtle is the small**est**.
3. There was a turtle call**ed** Shelly who was
   unhappy. She was cry**ing** one day, so
   Mitch the mouse rush**ed** over and told her
   a joke to make her laugh. Mitch and Shelly
   became best friend**s**, and Shelly was never
   sad again.

10-minute
Math

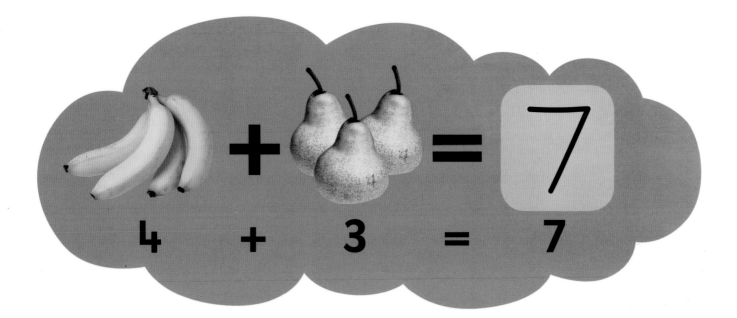

4 + 3 = 7

Addition

1 Count the strawberries and write the total in the box.

The **+** sign means **add**. The **=** sign means **equals**.

3 + 3 = 7

2 Count the apples and write the total in the box.

6 + 4 + 2 = 12

3 Now try these equations.

10 + 2 = 12

14 + 3 = 17

7 + 12 = 19

15 + 5 = 20

4 Sunil has five bananas.
Jess has three bananas.
How many do they have altogether?

8

24

Subtraction

1 Solve the equations below to find out how many spaceships are left.

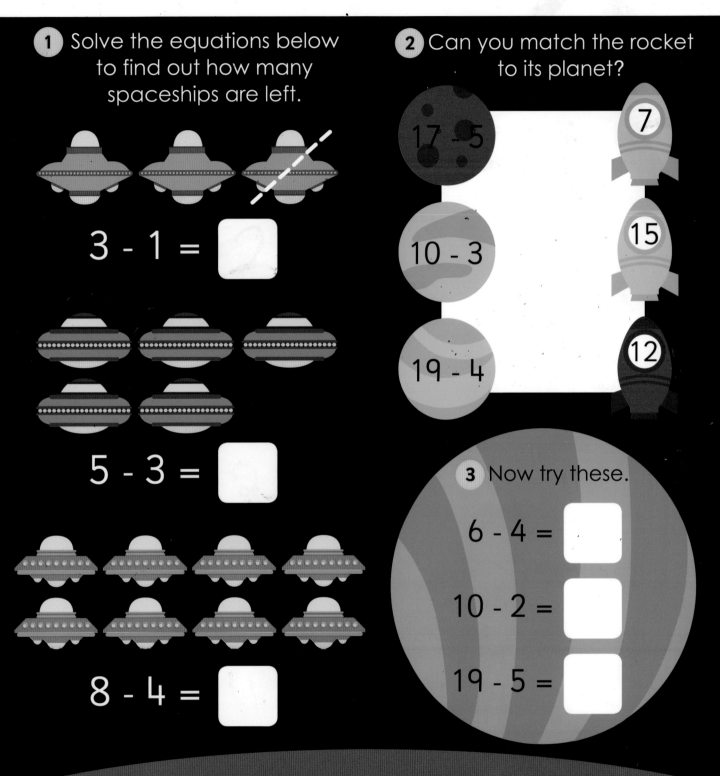

$3 - 1 =$ ☐

$5 - 3 =$ ☐

$8 - 4 =$ ☐

2 Can you match the rocket to its planet?

$17 - 5$

$10 - 3$

$19 - 4$

7

15

12

3 Now try these.

$6 - 4 =$ ☐

$10 - 2 =$ ☐

$19 - 5 =$ ☐

4 Seven aliens are flying to Earth. One gets lost on the way. How many make it to Earth? Write out the equation.

Don't forget the – and = signs!

Numbers

1 Write these numbers as words.

3 _____

9 _____

16 _____

2 Put these numbers in order from smallest to greatest.

48   13   37   22   65

[ ] [ ] [ ] [ ] [ ]

smallest   greatest

3 What comes next?

4   5   6   7   ___

18   19   20   21   ___

55   56   57   58   ___

4 Circle the flower with more petals.

5 There are twelve ducks in the pond. Four ducks fly away. How many ducks are left?

[ ] ducks

Making 10

1 Here are five ways to make 10. Swap them around to find five more. Copy the example.

10 + 0 = 10   0 + 10 = 10

9 + 1 = 10   ___ + ___ = ___

8 + 2 = 10   ___ + ___ = ___

7 + 3 = 10   ___ + ___ = ___

6 + 4 = 10   ___ + ___ = ___

2 These panda pairs together should add up to 10. Write in the missing numbers.

3 Cross out the animals that do not add up to 10.

4 Four little monkeys are given ten bananas. They eat one each. How many are left?

7 + 4

2 + 8

4 + 5

1 + 9

10 - ☐ = ☐

27

2-D shapes

1 Draw a robot from these shapes by following the instructions below.

1. His body has **4 sides all the same length.**
2. His head has **no corners.**
3. His legs and arms have **2 long sides and 2 short sides.**
4. His hands and feet have **3 corners.**
5. Well done! Now give him a face using triangles, squares, circles, and rectangles.

2 Cross out any shapes that are not triangles.

Measuring

1 Circle the shortest pencil.

2 Label these paint tubes 1 to 3, from shortest to tallest.

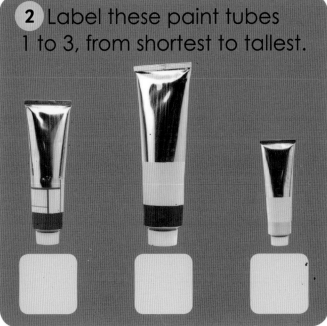

3 How many paper clips long is this paint palette?

paper clips

4 Which of these is the correct measurement of the paintbrush? Check the answer.

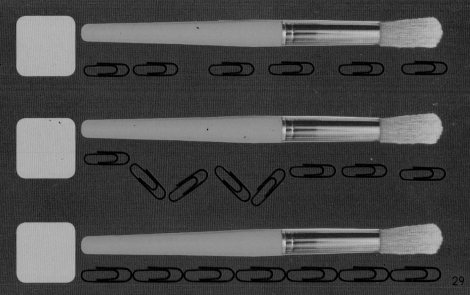

Time

1 Draw a line to match up the times with the clocks.

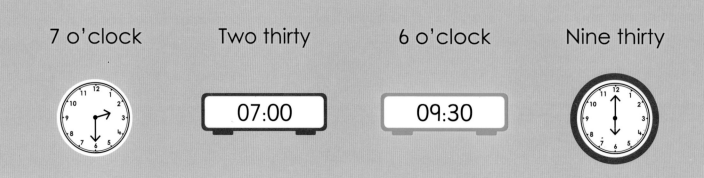

7 o'clock   Two thirty   6 o'clock   Nine thirty

07:00   09:30

2 What time is it?

_____ o'clock   _____ thirty

Remember, the little hand shows the hour.

3 School lunch is at half past 12. Draw the hands on the clock to show that it is lunchtime.

4 School finishes at 3 o'clock. Holly goes swimming one hour later. Check the time she goes swimming.

3 o'clock ☐

4 o'clock ☐

5 o'clock ☐

30

Counting by 2s and 5s

1 Use the clothesline of socks to help you count by 2s. Fill in the missing numbers.

| 2 | 4 | | | | | | | | |

2 Can you fill in the missing numbers on these scarves?

4
18
8
14
12
14

3 Use the fingers on these gloves to help you count by 5s and fill in the missing numbers.

| 5 | | | | 25 |

4 Jack and Helen have found some money in their pockets. How much do they have each?

☐ ¢

☐ ¢

5 Hats come in boxes of 5. Mr. May needs 30 hats for his class. How many boxes will he need?

5 hats

☐ boxes

31

3-D shapes

1 Circle the 3-D monsters. Hint: 3-D shapes are fat not flat!

2 Moz Monster is in his snack shelf.
Match each snack with the name of its shape.

cylinder   sphere   rectangular prism   cone

3 Moz is describing the shape of two things on the shelf. Name each shape.

a) "It is silver. The top and base are flat. You can roll it."

b) "It has 8 corners and 6 sides."

4 These squares will make a 3-D shape. What shape is it? Put a check next to your answer.

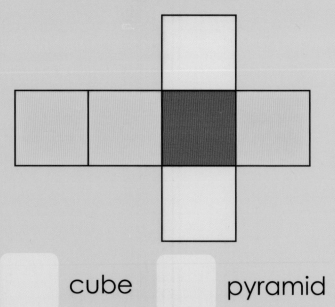

cube   pyramid

Halves and quarters

1 Help the baker cut each cookie into equal halves.

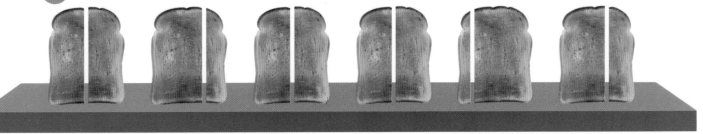

2 Circle the toast slices that have been cut in half fairly.

3 Cut these pizzas into quarters.

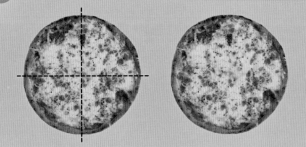

4 Circle the tomatoes that have been cut into quarters fairly.

5 Divide the pizza into four equal shares. Fill one quarter with cheese, one quarter with mushrooms, and two quarters with pepperoni.

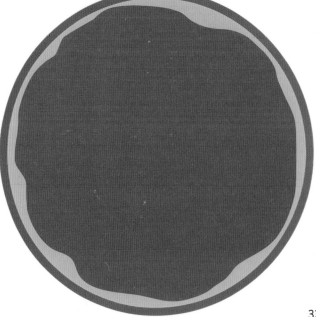

cheese   pepperoni   mushroom

Number problems

1 Fill in the missing numbers for these addition equations.

$3 + \boxed{} = 5$

$7 + \boxed{} = 11$

$12 + \boxed{} = 18$

$\boxed{} + 2 = 13$

2 Put a check next to the equations that are correct.

$11 + 7 = 20$ ☐

$3 + 6 = 9$ ☐

$12 + 5 = 17$ ☐

$18 - 3 = 12$ ☐

$18 - 6 = 12$ ☐

Use the number line, if you need to.

3 Fill in the missing numbers for these subtraction equations.

$14 - \boxed{} = 13$

$20 - \boxed{} = 16$

$9 - \boxed{} = 6$

$\boxed{} - 3 = 1$

4 Pirate Pete says 6 + 3 is the same as 3 + 6. Is he right? Can you prove it below?

Place value

1 Straws are sold in groups of ten, but there are some extras. How many straws are there in total?

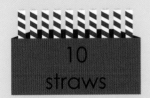
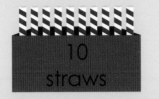
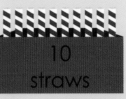

10 straws   10 straws   10 straws

2 Fill in the table for the other three numbers.

27

Tens	Ones
2	7

70

Tens	Ones

56

Tens	Ones

43

Tens	Ones

3 Put these numbers in order from smallest to greatest.

31   42   34   36   40

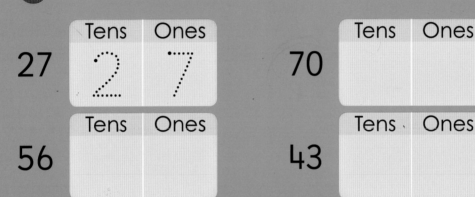

4 Rowan sold 38 milk shakes on Friday. The next day he sold 10 more. How many did he sell?

Counting by 10s

1 Farmer Phil sells eggs in boxes of 10. How many eggs are there?

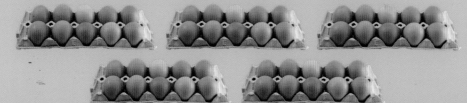

2 Jim needs 16 eggs. How many boxes will he need to buy?

How many eggs will he have left over?

3 Continue these number sequences.

14   24   34   ___   ___   ___   ___

98   88   78   68   ___   ___   ___

27   37   47   ___   ___   ___   ___

> Remember, we do not always have to start at 10 when we count in 10s.

4 Potatoes must be put in sacks of 10. There are 30 potatoes. How many sacks will we need?

5 Record 10 more than each number.

10 more

23

44

63

Money

1 Circle the coin that is worth the most.

2 How much money do you need to buy one orange and one apple?

10¢   8¢

◻ ¢

4 What is the total amount in each piggy bank?

3 Check the two equations that make 15¢.

12¢ + 3¢

16¢ - 2¢

20¢ - 5¢

◻ ¢

◻ ¢

◻ ¢

Use real money to help you, if you need to.

5 Tom has 16¢ to spend at the store. He gives half to Jack. How much money will they have each?

Tom will have ◻ ¢.

Jack will have ◻ ¢.

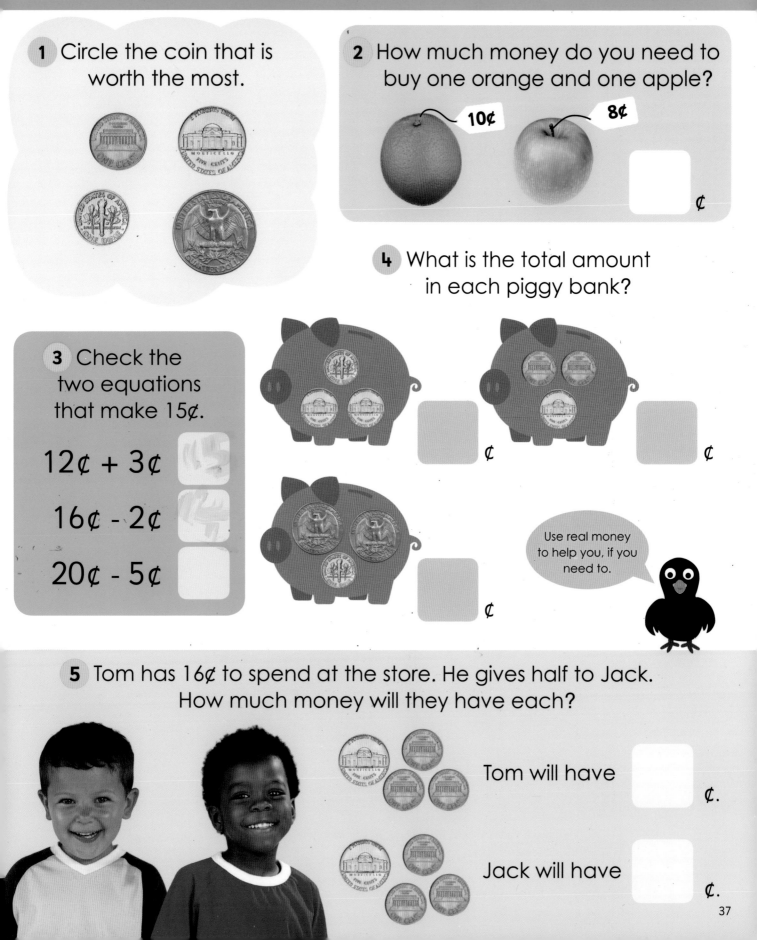

37

Addition to 20

1 Here are some ways of making 20. Can you swap the numbers around to find some other ways? The first one has been done for you.

15 + 5 = 20 $\underline{5}$ + $\underline{15}$ = $\underline{20}$ 16 + 4 = 20   _____ + _____ = _____

12 + 8 = 20   _____ + _____ = _____   2 + 18 = 20   _____ + _____ = _____

2 When you add the numbers on the turtles together, they must make 20. Cross out any pairs that are not correct.

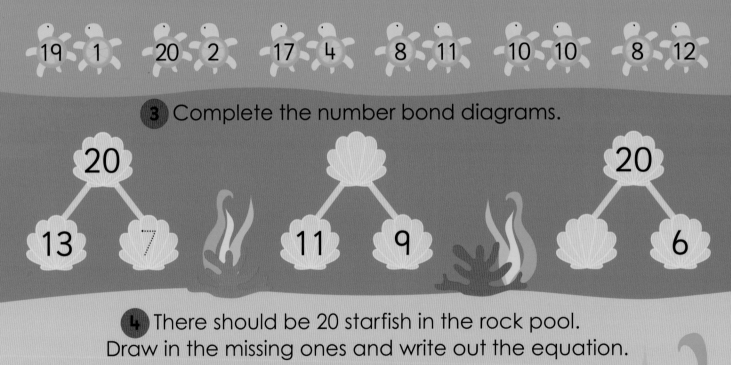

19 1   20 2   17 4   8 11   10 10   8 12

3 Complete the number bond diagrams.

20
13   7

9
11

20
6

4 There should be 20 starfish in the rock pool.
Draw in the missing ones and write out the equation.

Subtraction to 20

1 Here are two rows of bugs. How many are left in each row when three fly away?

$$12 - 3 = \boxed{}$$

Write out the equation. ▭

2 Now try these.

$15 - 7 = \boxed{}$

$19 - 5 = \boxed{}$

$14 - 8 = \boxed{}$

3 Can you match each bug to its leaf?

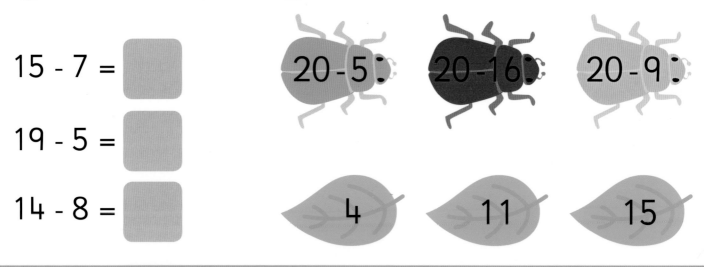

20 - 5 :   20 - 16 :   20 - 9 :

4   11   15

4 The red ladybug has 20 spots. The yellow ladybug has 16 spots. How many more spots does the red ladybug have?

Equations

1 Fill in the answers to the equations below.
Use this candy array to help you.

If you know 16 + 4 = 20, then you know that

20 – 4 = ⬜ and 20 – 16 = ⬜ .

2 Fill in the blanks in these related equations.

a   12 + 5 = ⬜   ⬜ – 5 = 12   ⬜ – 12 = 5

b   8 + 7 = ⬜   ⬜ – 8 = 7   ⬜ – 7 = 8

c   9 + ⬜ = 14   14 – 9 = ⬜   14 – ⬜ = 9

3 John has a bag containing 20 pieces of candy. He eats all the blue candy.

How many pieces of red candy are left in the bag? Write the equation below.

4 If you add the red and the blue candy together, how many pieces of candy are there?
Write the equation below.

Wipe any mistakes away and try again!

Equations to 100

1 Ali collects toy cars. He has 28. For his birthday, he gets 7 more. How many cars does Ali have now?
Show your work below.

2 Ali's friend Ella collects dinosaurs. Ali agrees to swap 10 of his cars for 10 of Ella's dinosaurs. How many cars does Ali have now? Show your work below.

3 Can you complete these equations?

33 + 2 = ☐   48 + 1 = ☐   21 + 5 = ☐   93 + 7 = ☐

4 Ali now has 10 dinosaurs. Ella has 50! How many more dinosaurs does Ella have than Ali?

Data

1 Safiya is selling fruit at a fair. Below are all the apples Safiya sold. Count the number of apples and complete the table.

Fruit	Number sold
Green apples	
Red apples	
Oranges	10
Bananas	5

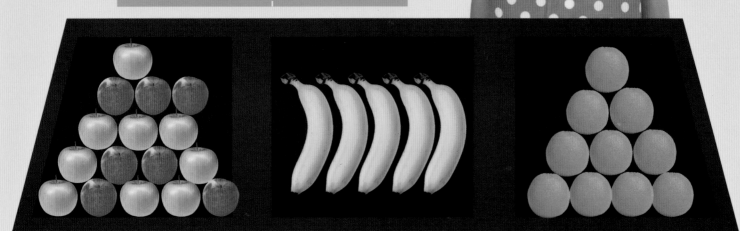

2 Using the data in the table, answer the following questions:

a) How many pieces of fruit did Safiya sell in total?

b) What is the difference between the number of red and green apples sold?

c) How many more apples than oranges did Safiya sell?

Answers

There are number games and flash cards at the back of the book.

Page 24 – Addition

1. $3 + 1 + 3 = \underline{7}$
2. $6 + 4 + 2 = \underline{12}$
3. $10 + 2 = \underline{12}$ $14 + 3 = \underline{17}$
   $7 + 12 = \underline{19}$ $15 + 5 = \underline{20}$
4. 8

Page 25 – Subtraction

1. $3 - 1 = \underline{2}$, $5 - 3 = \underline{2}$, $8 - 4 = \underline{4}$
2.

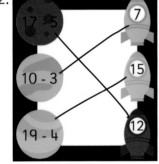

3. $6 - 4 = \underline{2}$
   $10 - 2 = \underline{8}$
   $19 - 5 = \underline{14}$
4. $7 - 1 = 6$

Page 26 – Numbers

1. three   nine   sixteen
2. 13 22 37 48 65
3. $\underline{8}$, $\underline{22}$, $\underline{59}$
4.

5. 8 ducks

Page 27 – Making 10

1. $1 + 9 = 10$ $2 + 8 = 10$
   $3 + 7 = 10$ $4 + 6 = 10$
2. 7 5

3.

4. $10 - \underline{4} = \underline{6}$

Page 28 – 2-D shapes

1.

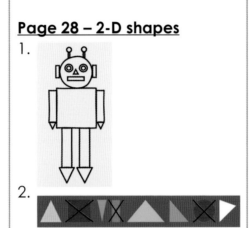

2.

Page 29 – Measuring

1.

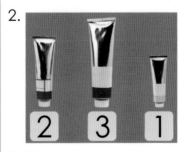

2.

2 3 1

3. 9
4.

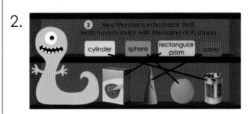

Page 30 – Time

1.

2. 3 o'clock   Seven thirty

3.

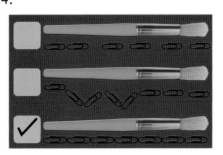

4. She goes swimming at **4 o'clock.**

Page 31 – Counting by 2s and 5s

1. 2 4 $\underline{6}$ $\underline{8}$ $\underline{10}$ $\underline{12}$ $\underline{14}$ $\underline{16}$ $\underline{18}$ $\underline{20}$
2. green scarf: $\underline{6}$
   yellow scarf: $\underline{16}$
   red scarf: $\underline{10}$
3. 5 $\underline{10}$ $\underline{15}$ $\underline{20}$ 25
4. 40¢, 25¢
5. 6 boxes

Page 32 – 3-D shapes

1.

2.

3. a) cylinder
   b) rectangular prism

4. cube

43

Page 33 – Halves and quarters

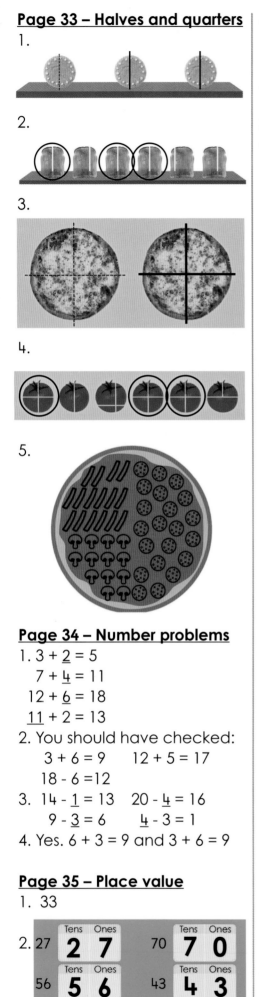

1.

2.

3.

4.

5.

Page 34 – Number problems

1. 3 + <u>2</u> = 5
   7 + <u>4</u> = 11
   12 + <u>6</u> = 18
   <u>11</u> + 2 = 13
2. You should have checked:
   3 + 6 = 9   12 + 5 = 17
   18 - 6 = 12
3. 14 - <u>1</u> = 13   20 - <u>4</u> = 16
   9 - <u>3</u> = 6   <u>4</u> - 3 = 1
4. Yes. 6 + 3 = 9 and 3 + 6 = 9

Page 35 – Place value

1. 33

2. 27

	Tens	Ones
	2	**7**

70

	Tens	Ones
	7	**0**

56

	Tens	Ones
	5	**6**

43

	Tens	Ones
	4	**3**

3. 31 34 36 40 42
4. 48

Page 36 – Counting by 10s

1. 50
2. 2, 4
3. 14 24 34 <u>44</u> <u>54</u> <u>64</u> <u>74</u>
   98 88 78 68 <u>58</u> <u>48</u> <u>38</u>
   27 37 47 <u>57</u> <u>67</u> <u>77</u> <u>87</u>
4. 3
5.

23	10 more	**33**
44		**54**
63		**73**

Page 37 – Money

1.

2. 18¢
3. You should have checked:
   12¢ + 3¢ and 20¢ - 5¢
4. 20¢, 7¢, 60¢
5. Tom will have 8¢
   Jack will have 8¢

Page 38 – Addition to 20

1. 8 + 12 = 20
   4 + 16 = 20
   18 + 2 = 20
2.
3.
   20 → 11 / 9   20 → **14** / 6
4. 13 + 7 = 20

Page 39 – Subtraction to 20

1. 9
   14 - 3 = 11
2. 15 - 7 = <u>8</u>

19 - 5 = <u>14</u>
14 - 8 = <u>6</u>

3.
   20 - 5 → 15
   20 - 16 → 4
   20 - 9 → 11

4. 20 - 16 = 4

Page 40 – Equations

1. 20 - 4 = <u>16</u>
   20 - 16 = <u>4</u>
2. a) 12 + 5 = <u>17</u>
       <u>17</u> - 5 = 12
       <u>17</u> - 12 = <u>5</u>
   b) 8 + 7 = <u>15</u>
       <u>15</u> - 8 = 7
       <u>15</u> - 7 = 8
   c) 9 + <u>5</u> = 14
       14 - 9 = <u>5</u>
       14 - <u>5</u> = 9
3. 20 - 8 = 12
4. 8 + 12 = 20

Page 41 – Equations to 100

1. 28 + 7 = 35
2. 35 - 10 = 25
3. 33 + 2 = 35   48 + 1 = 49
   21 + 5 = 26   93 + 7 = 100
4. 40

Page 42 – Data

1.

Fruit	Number sold
Green apples	**9**
Red apples	**7**
Oranges	10
Bananas	5

2. a) 31
   b) 2
   c) 6

Word cards

For games, see inside the back cover.

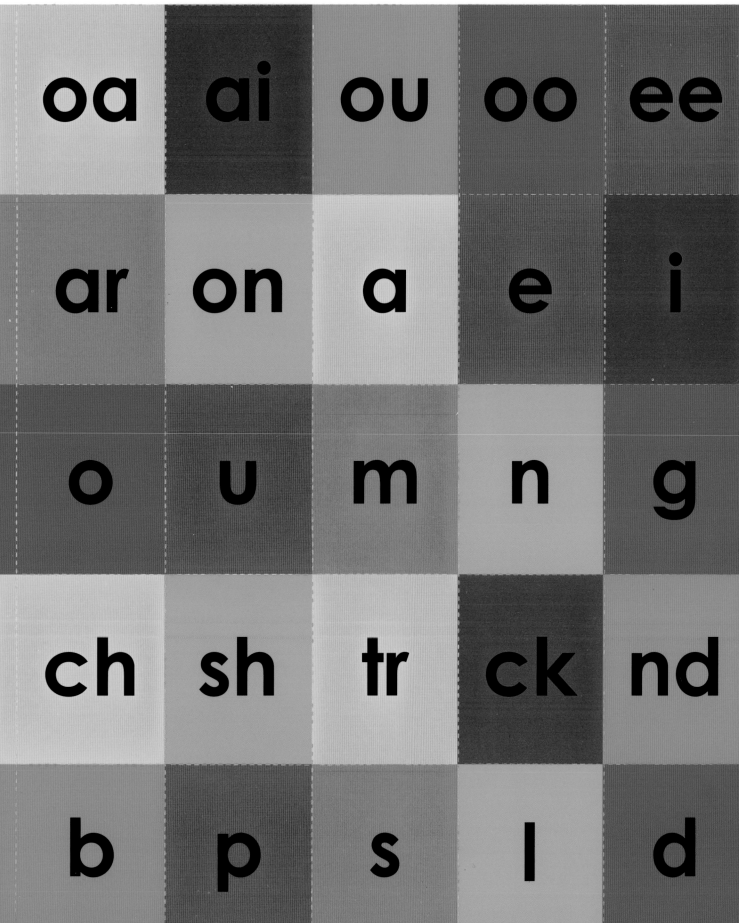

oa ai ou oo ee

ar on a e i

o u m n g

ch sh tr ck nd

b p s l d

Number cards

For games, see inside the back cover.

1 2 3 4 5

6 7 8 9 10

1 2 3 4 5

6 7 8 9 10

0 0 + - =